A Director's Guide

Reputation management

STRATEGIES FOR PROTECTING COMPANIES, THEIR BRANDS AND THEIR DIRECTORS

Editor, Director Publications: Tom Nash
Managing Editor: Lesley Shutte
Production Manager: Victoria Davies
Design: Halo Design
Commercial Director: Simon Seward
Managing Director: Andrew Main Wilson
Chairman: Tim Melville-Ross

Published for the Institute of Directors
and AIG Europe (UK) Limited
by Director Publications Ltd
116 Pall Mall London SW1Y 5ED

Editorial: 0171 766 8910
Production: 0171 766 8960
Sponsorship: 0171 766 8885
Copy sales: 0171 766 8960
Facsimile: 0171 766 8990

© Copyright March 1999
Director Publications Ltd

Price £9.95

YOURS TO HAVE AND TO HOLD
BUT NOT TO COPY

The publication you are reading is protected by copyright law. This means that the publisher could take you and your employer to court and claim heavy legal damages if you make unauthorised photocopies from these pages. Photocopying copyright material without permission is no different from stealing a magazine from a newsagent.

The Copyright Licensing Agency (CLA) issues licences to bring photocopying within the law. It has designed licensing services to cover all kinds of special needs in business, education and government.

If you take photocopies from books, magazines and periodicals at work your employer should be licensed with the CLA. Make sure you are protected by a photocopying licence.

The Copyright Licensing Agency
90 Tottenham Court Road
London W1P 0LP
Tel: 0171 436 5931 Fax: 0171 436 3986

Apart from any fair dealing for the purposes of research or private study, or criticism or review, as permitted under the Copyright, Designs and Patents Act, 1988, this publication may only be reproduced, stored or transmitted, in any form or by any means, with the prior permission in writing of the publishers or, in the case of reprographic reproduction, in accordance with the terms and licences issued by the CLA. Enquiries concerning the reproduction outside those terms should be sent to the publishers at the undermentioned addresses:

Director Publications Ltd
116 Pall Mall
London SW1Y 5ED

Kogan Page Ltd
120 Pentonville Road
London N1 9JN

© Director Publications 1999

British Library Cataloguing in Publication Data
A CIP record for this book is available from the British Library
ISBN 0 7494 3030 3

Printed and bound in Great Britain by St Ives plc

Contents

What is
the only thing
more important
than your
reputation?

Protecting it.

 The power in business insurance

Planning for the worst

Tim Melville-Ross, Director General, Institute of Directors

For the benefit of any directors who remain sceptical about the power of this intangible asset called "reputation", let me start with a brief anecdote.

A few years ago a crowded bus broke down outside a bank in central Hong Kong. There was absolutely nothing wrong with the bank – it was the bus that had broken down – but some quite frightening consequences flowed from the bus passengers milling around on the pavement while they waited for someone to come and fix the bus. Other passers-by saw a large group of people outside the bank branch, and rumours started to spread that the bank was crowded with people wanting to take their money out. Before long, every other branch of the bank in Hong Kong was being besieged by customers wanting to withdraw their money.

I recount this story because it is a good example of the sort of reputation-threatening incident that rapidly turns into a crisis. It is also the sort of misfortune for which, you might imagine, even a seriously competent management team could not be expected to prepare. But there I would disagree. Although it is not possible to know the source of every potential threat to a business, it is possible – indeed essential – to plan for the worst.

The management of its own reputation is a vital issue for any company. It is the responsibility of directors to ensure the issues are fully understood at board level and that time is spent identifying reputational risks and putting in place thorough, but flexible, plans to deal with them. This guide will assist them in discharging that responsibility.

Reputation: rhetoric versus reality

Michael L Sherman, Chief Operating Officer, AIG Europe (UK) Limited

In an era in which competition for scarce resources and market leadership is fiercer than ever, directors and managers are realising that a good corporate reputation is worth its weight in gold.

The proof is hard to deny. Surveys of the "world's most admired companies" are accompanied by analysts espousing the tangible benefits – and diminished risk – of investing in both large and small companies with robust reputations. Reports on reputation and what it contributes to the bottom line have moved rapidly out of the pages of specialist marketing media and onto the business pages. Strategies on how to create, cultivate and protect this elusive asset have now made it to the top of boardroom agendas in almost all industries.

AIG Europe is delighted to be sponsoring this Director's Guide on reputation, which provides some valuable insights and practical advice for directors of companies of all sizes. It covers such key issues as the role reputation plays in sound corporate governance, how to evaluate its contribution as an asset, and how to harness it when a large-scale crisis threatens to turn the tide against your company.

The range of subjects covered and the diverse backgrounds of the authors who have contributed reflect the 360-degree approach that AIG Europe recommends companies adopt to assess and respond to the virtues and vulnerabilities of reputation.

Reputation management is no longer rhetoric – it's reality. Like most things in business, there is no magic bullet to make it work. However, companies that make it a genuine priority and play a long-term game will be the winners. The overall message is clear: a focused strategy and real investment will help companies not only create and maintain reputation, but also build on it, repair it and capitalise on it when times are troubled. No other company asset – visible or invisible – has such profound power to make or break a company's viability.

Reputation.

The only
thing that can
give your business
a second chance.

 **The power in business insurance**

Chapter 1

Making the most of your reputation

Michael L Sherman, chief operating officer, AIG Europe (UK) Limited, says that companies are only just beginning to value their reputation – and to invest in it

"If we lost all of our production facilities, we could rebuild the business. But if we lost our brand name and reputation, the business would collapse." So says the chief executive of a leading, UK consumer goods manufacturer.

Businesses have traditionally placed a higher value on the tangible than the intangible. Only now are companies starting to recognise that the focus on financial assets has been at the expense of the intangible asset with – arguably – the greatest potential to jeopardise the viability of a business if neglected: corporate reputation.

Until now, the approach to managing corporate reputation has been less than scientific. But the practice of reputation management is now being looked at in a new light. More companies are converting to "reputation religion" as they experience first-hand the advantages of a strong reputation and the drawbacks of a weak one.

Directors, chief executives and managers have now realised that even the best-intentioned philanthropic efforts and ad hoc sponsorships are not enough to cultivate a solid reputation. It's like everything else in business – unless you invest in it, cultivate it and approach it as conscientiously as you would an addition to the product portfolio, it will not be there to facilitate business success or cushion the business during a crisis.

WHAT ARE THE BENEFITS?

Although it is difficult to pinpoint the exact financial value of a good reputation to a business, the benefits are clear-cut for companies of any size in any sector. A good reputation can:

■ *Create barriers to competition and inhibit the mobility of rival companies;*

■ *Attract the best recruits and therefore help avert skill shortages;*

■ *Attract the best supply chain and business partners;*

■ *Enhance access to capital and attract investors;*

■ *Open doors to new markets;*

■ *Create a "premium" value for a company's products and services; and*

■ *Protect the business in times of crisis.*

As a result of these benefits, reputation is fast becoming the most coveted, if least understood, of all corporate assets. It is set to play a key role in the way businesses are built in the future.

WHAT DRIVES REPUTATION?

According to research by MORI and *Fortune* magazine, there are seven key drivers of corporate reputation:

■ *Financial performance, profitability and long-term investment value;*

■ *The chief executive and senior management team;*

■ *Quality of products and services;*

■ *Treatment of staff;*

■ *Social responsibility;*

■ *Customer service; and*

■ *Ability to communicate.*

The findings on the previous page show that all areas of a business contribute to corporate reputation – it is not just a public relations issue. If image is the immediate external perception of an organisation, it could be argued that reputation is the historic and cultural dimension of that image – a stakeholder community's "social memory" of the sum total of a company and its activities.

Reputation is a by-product of the intersection between a company's values and the values of the society in which it operates. Organisations that are out of step with the attitudes of audiences at a given point in time are unlikely to enjoy a positive reputation. The key is the "crossover factor": unless the values intersect, the company could sustain reputation damage.

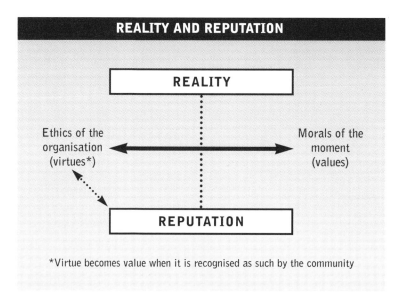

REALITY AND REPUTATION

REALITY

Ethics of the organisation (virtues*) ←————→ Morals of the moment (values)

REPUTATION

*Virtue becomes value when it is recognised as such by the community

REPUTATION'S PLACE ON A CROWDED BUSINESS AGENDA

Today, the challenges for business managers – whatever the size of their company – are immense. They are required to lead massive organisational changes and face unremitting pressure to streamline costs.

Regulators, pressure groups and consumers are all scrutinising company activities and raising the bar for corporate ethics.

Employees, though less loyal, are also more demanding of the organisations they work for.

These factors – vying with each other against a backdrop of social change and technological advancement – are exerting unprecedented pressure on political and consumer groups' agendas. This is why reputation has moved out of the public relations arena and into the boardroom. In markets where companies are having to strive harder and harder to secure increasingly scarce resources and more demanding customers, reputation has the potential to be the single differentiating factor between a company and its competitors.

TRANSPARENCY, CONSISTENCY AND ACCOUNTABILITY

One of the most critical reasons for investing in reputation is that company stakeholders – customers, partners, investors, staff and suppliers – expect more than ever before. A company's ability to meet these expectations has a significant impact on its profitability, its capacity to grow and indeed its overall viability.

Consumers are now more business-literate than in the past, and investors want to see more than just a roll-call of healthy tangible assets before they take an equity stake in a company. How stakeholders perceive reputation has become a front-line issue. It's now accepted by the business community that consumers are often reticent about buying products and services from companies with a dubious reputation.

A strong reputation can also serve as an agent for positive change and better performance. More and more companies are using the strength of their corporate reputation in their product marketing and advertising. It is a cohesive umbrella that provides customers with a tacit guarantee about the quality and value of a product.

This corporate halo effect is particularly key in markets where it is difficult to differentiate a product or service. When customers are faced with two products or services of equivalent value, the intangible reassurance of a reputable company backing the offer can be the deciding factor.

REPUTATION ON THE LINE

An event can become a crisis because it threatens a company's short-term prospects and, if the event is mismanaged, its long-term survival. Companies rely on delicate inter-relationships for their mandate to operate. When these relationships are jolted – and profitability threatened – by an internally or externally generated disaster, companies with a strong reputation that act quickly to maintain stakeholder confidence, underpin sales, protect their market position and communicate with regulators will be the companies that go furthest toward guarding shareholder value.

Conversely, companies with dented reputations are likely to find it harder to attract investment, retain customers and employees and compete in chosen markets.

A damaged corporate reputation can often be repaired or rebuilt, but ongoing nurturing of reputation can prevent the need for this. Many companies have discovered that a well of goodwill among consumers, the media, suppliers, investors and the community – earned through years of understanding and meeting the needs of all these audiences at different times – can soften the detrimental impact a crisis has on their reputation.

In the past few years, the media coverage of business and political issues has grown enormously – so no business can expect to escape unwanted media attention during a crisis. The best defence is not only to be prepared, but also to have built up a substantial bank of goodwill with each stakeholder group over time. This can be powerful enough to secure a second chance for companies even after a catastrophe.

A STRONG REPUTATION MEANS A STRONG BUSINESS

Investing in reputation management is an investment in the future of a company. Historically, good reputations are sound indicators of solid financial performance.

For small and medium-sized companies, a robust reputation makes a difference when competing for capital, employees or customer loyalty. For example, a strong reputation can help smaller private companies when they seek finance for growth or look to

13

divest subsidiaries. All investors – from private individuals to banks to venture capitalists – are influenced by a company's standing in the marketplace. Investors are willing to pay more for equity in companies with a strong reputation than for a stake in less reputable companies which offer otherwise comparable risk and return. The more reputable the company, the lower the risk attached to its capital.

A recent study by New York University's Stern School of Business showed that companies with good reputations have a rate of profitability in excess of the industry average. The study also found that there is a relative premium on the stockmarket value of firms with stronger reputations for social responsibility, and that one-year corporate earnings-per-share forecasts made by financial analysts are partly influenced by the non-financial component of a company's reputation.

A strong corporate reputation also helped companies during the stockmarket crash of 1987. According to the Brouillard study based on *Fortune* magazine's 15th Annual Survey of America's most admired companies, shares in America's ten most admired public companies recovered faster and suffered less, while shares in ten of the least admired companies fell three times as far.

The real value of an equity stake in a private company, or shares in a publicly listed company, is increasingly greater than the total value of its assets. As with brands, an emotional factor often drives values above the financial worth of the investment.

THREE TYPES OF VALUE

Implicit within an investment stake in a company – regardless of whether it is a private or public entity – are three different types of value:

■   *Emotional value (investors' loyalty towards a company);*

■   *Trust value (the faith investors have in the directors of a company and their level of optimism about its business performance); and*

■   *Basic value (the redeemable financial value of the investment).*

These values combine to form the total worth – above and beyond the asset value – that a stake in a company represents to its investors. And reputation is a crucial element in each of them.

INVESTING IN REPUTATION

Measuring reputation can provide a good barometer of the sustained value of a company. This intangible asset may well constitute a more enduring source of competitive advantage than intellectual and physical property.

Despite the difficulty of valuing reputation and deciding what should be invested in developing and managing it, more companies have begun to realise that investment is vital. But they are only part of the way there. Only when companies make reputation management a consultative, inclusive process involving all areas of the business will they be able to converse with stakeholders in terms of real value – a language they understand.

Although the asset of a strong reputation doesn't appear on the balance sheet, it's the asset with arguably the greatest potential to make or break businesses. The sooner more business people understand the powerful fulcrum it provides when harnessed and managed, the sooner more of us will be able to turn it to our marketing advantage and lean on it in times of crisis.

Chapter 2

The good, the bad and the ugly

PART ONE: REPUTATIONS CAN BE A DOUBLE-EDGED SWORD

Mark Watson, corporate governance executive, Institute of Directors, advises on the steps that directors should take at board level to protect their reputation and that of their company

A company's reputation can be its most important corporate asset. Good reputations can differentiate companies, generate brand loyalty and provide a cushion in times of difficulty. In competitive markets, it is the companies with the best-managed reputations that will have an edge. They will find it easier to attract investment and keep both customers and suppliers happy.

But imagine that as managing director of a company you get a police report stating that a batch of your best-selling medicine has been laced with cyanide and killed two people. Or that one of your foreign manufacturing plants released a deadly gas, killing untold numbers of people. Or, while less dramatic in human terms, but no less so for your company, allegations have been made that your car repair operations consistently overcharge your customers.

What the board does next, and how the company handles the crisis, will affect the company's reputation for years. In fact, your reputation may determine whether there is a company left. Yet, how often has your board considered the likely adverse effect of a crisis on your company's reputation and how this might affect your relationship with your key stakeholders – the shareholders, staff, suppliers, customers, partners and investors?

In the first part of this chapter, we explore what might be done to avoid the kinds of disaster that are highlighted in the second part. While Chapter 5 pinpoints some of the things that should be done once a crisis has occurred, here we try to highlight how one might take some pre-emptive action to avoid or lessen the potential impact of a crisis on one of your company's most valued assets – its reputation.

PREVENTION IS THE BEST MEDICINE

As the saying goes, prevention is better than cure. In business this is no less true. The best crisis management technique is to avoid the crisis in the first place. A board can do a lot to prevent a potentially disastrous situation before it arises.

First, examine the areas of greatest legal exposure and take steps to guard against problems. Rather than calling in the lawyers only after a problem has materialised, preventative action requires the board and its legal advisers to identify those areas where your company is most likely to face exposure in the future.

Even the smallest sensible actions can reap rewards in limiting a company's liability. For example, personal injury cases are sometimes won because the company had taken the time to teach employees how to react to and report workplace accidents.

Second, designate a director to whom employee, customer and public concerns can be addressed. This ensures that overall responsibility is given to an individual with sufficient clout to keep the issue as high profile as necessary.

Many times, even major crises could have been avoided if employees had been asked a single question before acting. To assist, everything possible must be done to address employee and public concerns internally, by providing a safe haven for reports of actual or potential problems and guaranteeing anonymity and freedom from retribution to those who file complaints.

Third, while no company can anticipate all legal challenges, it is, nonetheless, important to watch closely for changes in the law and adjust your practices accordingly.

Fourth, establish disclosure procedures which ensure that the picture emerging from the company's communications function parallels the reality perceived by those outside. Many companies have already taken such steps, including educating the board about the disclosure standards that apply to London Stock Exchange listed companies, and disclosing bad news early to minimise the surprise to the market.

The considerable liability that can result from any mis-statement is incentive enough for most boards to exercise caution in the disclosure process.

ANTICIPATING THE INEVITABLE

In spite of all this planning, it is still possible for a good company to find itself confronted with a bad situation, such as the act of a disgruntled employee or a natural disaster. So, it is not a bad plan to assume that something unfortunate will happen and therefore, in anticipation, do the following:

- *Identify and prepare a crisis management team;*

- *Formulate a crisis management plan;*

- *Remind board members that more is at stake than their own reputation.*

THE LONGER VIEW

While it might be human nature to keep problems quiet, there comes a point when the company needs to admit that it has a problem, indicate what it is doing to correct the situation and then make amends. Restoring customer confidence is far more important than wasting time devising a potential defence. After all, a defence is of little use if there is no company left to defend. Directors should, therefore, ask themselves how they would want to be treated if they were shareholders in the company and act accordingly.

Efforts to avoid crisis situations are, in a way, mundane matters and are unlikely to get a company acclaimed in the press. However, perhaps for that reason alone, it may be one of the most valuable tasks any board should undertake. The remainder of the chapter shows why.

PART TWO: REPUTATIONS UNDER FIRE

Alan Malachowski, business lecturer, University of East Anglia, examines some of the different ways in which reputations have been damaged

Reputation management is a difficult and complex task. In preparing for the unexpected, companies need to be familiar with the problems others have faced. The following are examples of cases where reputations have come under threat.

JEWELLER LOSES MORE THAN HIS SHINE

Hard-won reputations can be destroyed in the blink of a customer's eye. Ask Gerald Ratner. Everyone knows his story. It has entered the realms of business mythology. One minute Ratner was the world's largest and most popular jeweller, heading a very profitable international empire of well over two thousand shops. Then, a couple of jocular moments later, his company plunged £122m into the red as core customers rapidly lost faith in its products. Before long, Ratner himself was ousted from an organisation to which he had devoted the whole of his working life.

Ratner poked fun at the quality of his company's products in a highly public forum before some six thousand members of the Institute of Directors. He had made such remarks before. And since they had even been reported in *The Sun* and the *Financial Times*, he saw no harm in livening up the occasion by repeating them. But this time the press took his humour to task with a vengeance, and the results were commercially disastrous.

The plight of Ratner serves as a timely warning: reputations are fragile. But it was surely a one-off example of reputational meltdown. Short of a blanket insurance policy covering all eventualities, there seems to be little companies can do to avoid such occurrences. Hence the more interesting and more instructive cases in the long run are those in which it appears that something worthwhile could have been done.

FATAL FLAWS

The very phrase "corporate murder" conjures up images of ranting anti-business pressure groups.

Unfortunately, it now encapsulates a director's worst nightmare. "There is a growing realisation among insurers that not only could directors be prosecuted for manslaughter but companies could too," claims Lloyd's underwriter Reg Brown. Think of the massive legal fallout from major catastrophes like Bhopal and Piper Alpha. Better still, think of smaller-scale, less sensationalised disasters such as the fatal canoeing accident in Lyme Regis in March 1993 and the M2 coach crash in Kent which happened in the same year.

The sad deaths in Lyme Regis and on the M2 showed just how vulnerable small companies are. Misfortunes can be particularly damaging to these companies because their reputations depend so much on repeat business and word-of-mouth recommendations.

In the Lyme Regis case, a combination of poor management, human error and the unexpected force of the natural elements caused the tragic deaths of four teenagers from Southway Comprehensive School in Plymouth. What should have been a routine two-hour paddle to nearby Charmouth went horribly wrong when the canoes were swept out to sea in rough weather and swamped by freezing water.

The consequences for the St Albans Challenge Centre involved in the tragedy were also bleak. Managing Director Peter Kite was jailed on four charges of manslaughter and the company was fined £60,000. Nine months before the accident, Kite had been forewarned of possible dangers by two former employees. They told him that the activity centre lacked properly qualified staff and adequate equipment. Noting that that he had chosen to ignore these complaints, Mr Justice Ognall told Kite during his trial at Winchester Crown Court that he had been "more interested in sales than safety".

Similar themes of negligence, error and mismanagement run through the case of the M2 coach crash. A day trip to Canterbury Cathedral and Leeds Castle near Maidstone in Kent ended in disaster when a coach operated by Travellers Coach Company careered off the motorway and down an embankment, killing nine of the American tourists on board as well as the driver.

The inquest was informed that the tachograph showed the coach had been travelling at 78mph, that the compulsory 70mph speed-limiter on the coach had been disconnected and that its anti-lock braking system and designated warning light were faulty. A verdict of unlawful killing was returned by the jury. In view of this the coroner for East Kent indicated that he would shortly be referring the case to the Crown Prosecution Service.

GREEN IMAGE RECEIVES A BODY BLOW

All companies are ethically required to try to ensure that they do not cause or contribute to accidents. But sometimes a company's own reputation for ethical correctness can trigger criticism. The Body Shop and Ben & Jerry's are leading lights in the field of ethical corporate awareness. Both have suffered severe damage to their reputation in recent years.

From modest beginnings in a Brighton cosmetic shop in 1976, the Roddicks built the Body Shop into a multinational company with over 1,400 retail outlets in 45 countries.

In the process, Anita Roddick amassed an estimated personal fortune of over £150m. But money was never supposed to be the motivating factor. The Body Shop was in business to fulfil an ethical agenda which included: fostering human rights, promoting environmentally-friendly products and bolstering the economies and self-esteem of the so-called Third World.

Consumers apparently liked this agenda and voted for it with their purses. But, when journalists began to question the chorus of publicity in praise of the Body Shop's ethical image, the tide of enthusiasm started to turn. For some journalists, most notably Jon Entine, claimed that the image did not stand up to scrutiny.

In September 1994, US magazine *Business Ethics* published Entine's controversial article *Shattered image: is the Body Shop too good to be true?* It attacked the Body Shop's reputation on all fronts. According to Entine, many of the Body Shop's products failed to live up to their reputation for naturalness, using only microscopic and ineffective levels of botanical extracts in contrast to much larger quantities of petrochemical ingredients. He argued, furthermore, that the whole franchise operation was beset with problems and had been intensively investigated for fraud.

Entine also cited grave ethical difficulties with some of the Body Shop's projects in developing countries. He maintained that micro-schemes involving the Pueblo Indians in the US and natives in Tanzania and the Solomon Islands had all been beset with problems. Finally, he drew attention to the image-destroying fact that the Body Shop seemed to have given no money to charity in its first 11 years and far less than the average company over its entire history.

Unless they are conclusively refuted, such harsh claims can only harm a company's reputation. But while the Body Shop wobbled between threats and denials, other writers joined the fray. Even though the Body Shop's image may not be shattered as Entine maintained, it is now subject to uncomfortably hostile worldwide scrutiny by journalists and academics.

A WASTED OPPORTUNITY

Ben & Jerry's was founded in 1978 by two young men, Ben Cohen and Jerry Greenfield, who were making ice cream in their own kitchen. From these humble beginnings, the duo went on to produce a national brand, and in 1984 their company went public.

By 1992, the company's revenues had reached $131m. It employed 350 people and managed to capture a 36 per cent share of the premium ice cream market where Häagen-Dazs was the main competitor. This rapid growth was particularly impressive for newcomers in a mature industry where consumption of ice cream had tended to remain constant and looked likely to suffer a slight decline.

The founders were idealists and saw themselves as children of the sixties, when social activism and environmentalism were popular. They had started the company with the intention of not only making profits, but also promoting social causes. Their green vision included a product mission, a social mission and an economic mission. When Ben & Jerry's came up with the idea of giving the waste from their Vermont ice cream-producing operation to local farmers, this looked like yet another progressive move in their well-known policy of idiosyncratic benevolence.

At first it seemed like a win-win situation: Ben & Jerry's would avoid a small environmental difficulty and the farmers would get a bonus of diluted ice cream for their pigs. At least that was how the story was initially played out in the media.

SWINEGATE

But when the ice cream-fed pigs suddenly began to die of uncannily human-like arteriosclerosis at a full 400lbs short of their expected adult weight, a problem loomed.

Ben & Jerry's would probably have been forgiven if they had simply come clean. After all, their original idea was well-intentioned and the outcome unforeseeable. But they foolishly tried to cover things up and thereby precipitated an unnecessary reputational crisis – a mini "swinegate". Reference to the project was erased from the company's annual report and even the social auditor was forbidden to speak about it.

Like the Body Shop, Ben & Jerry's was seen to be acting against the whole spirit of its reputation for ethical awareness. Therefore it is not surprising that this reputation soon came back to haunt the company.

Chapter 3

Valuing corporate reputation

Shailendra Kumar, senior consultant, brand valuation, at Interbrand Newell and Sorrell, stresses that while putting a value on corporate reputation is not easy, it can be done

The importance of corporate reputation and the corporate brand is clear and one is inextricably linked to the other. Corporate reputation is the overall perception held by the organisation's key stakeholders, the media and the public. The corporate brand is the means by which this reputation is communicated and is the organisation's promise in the minds of all stakeholders.

Favourable reputations (as embodied in the corporate brand) produce tangible benefits. A favourable reputation can deliver:

- *Premium prices for products;*

- *Lower costs of capital and labour;*

- *A buffer zone of goodwill in the event of crisis;*

- *Improved loyalty from employees and customers.*

It is this last area which is most important, instigating the virtuous circle of corporate branding. Motivated employees provide good service, which precipitates repeat custom, which enhances the value of the corporate brand, which attracts the best employees and so on. This is a noble enough objective and explains companies' obsession with reputation. But to fully understand the rise of corporate branding we need to take a step back to its roots.

Today, customers are far more sophisticated than they used to be. In markets where there is access to increasing levels of information there is an opportunity to disseminate more and more data. Putting this in a business context means that greater competition and ease of technology has rendered erstwhile points of differentiation – such as price and product and service quality – today's points of parity. The battleground for differentiation is often fought at the next level up – the corporate level. Pressure for corporate responsibility and accountability has been given momentum by lobby groups, the government and a social conscience born of greater awareness.

Today's companies can expect the keen eye of scrutiny to bear down on their reputation through every activity. Environmentalists caused a media frenzy forcing Shell to change its proposed plans for the dumping of the Brent Spa oil rig in the North Sea. Nike has risen like a colossus in the corporate brand world but along with that elevated status have come allegations about the exploitation of Third World child labour. McDonald's, one of the world's leading brands, came under severe attack for its involvement with the destruction of Brazilian rainforests.

FINANCIAL LOSS

The loss of corporate reputation can be quickly felt in financial terms on the world's stockmarkets. When the Exxon Valdez spilt its crude load off the Alaskan coast, the estimated cost of the clean-up and the settlement of lawsuits that ensued was more than $2.5bn. In addition, the public relations disaster that followed saw five per cent ($3bn) of Exxon's stockmarket value wiped out.

However, others have applied reputation management as part of a conscious business proposition. The Co-operative Bank has used the new social conscience as a basis on which to develop a brand strategy and an ethos for its existence. Its policy of ethical invest-ment has reaped handsome rewards in terms of account openings and credit card applications. Forty-four per cent of new account openings were claimed as due to the bank's ethical positioning and, today, the Co-operative Bank is the largest issuer of Gold Visa cards in Europe.

Most importantly it has given the bank a strong brand platform and a differentiated offering with which it is building its reputation. In a recent survey by Corporate Edge, 65 per cent of respondents supported the decision of supermarket chain Iceland not to stock genetically engineered food. More than a quarter said they would actively choose to shop at Iceland as a result. But beware, consumers are not always easily persuaded. The same survey revealed that 65 per cent perceived corporate support for green issues to be no more than a cynical marketing ploy.

BRAND STRATEGY

Many companies apply a monolithic brand strategy where the product or service brand is also the corporate brand. Examples are Marks & Spencer, Coca-Cola, IBM, British Airways and Virgin. In these cases the reputation of the corporate brand is built in part through the products and services that bear the same brand name.

Such companies enjoy the advantages of cheaper brand building, instant credibility for brand extensions and the seamless transfer of reputation. The latter is, of course, a double-edged sword. The seamless transfer of reputation runs in both directions, good and bad. Good reputation is built on sound financial performance, creating shareholder value and meeting City expectations – things that are easily measurable. But reputation is also built through an organisation's ability to satisfy all of its stakeholders, which, in the context of reputation, will also include the public at large.

Those factors which contribute to the development of corporate reputation include the organisation's stance on the environment, health and safety, corporate governance and even human rights and the respect for local culture and communities. Shell's reputation was again in tatters when it found itself embroiled in Nigerian civil unrest – especially after the assassination of Ken Saro-Wiwa who had opposed Shell's activities in the West African state.

The ability of organisations to manage their reputation is critically dependent upon their ability to communicate with their stakeholders and the audience at large. The newly privatised utilities and the National Lottery suffered at the hands of the "fat cats" debacle partly because their management had not maintained a public service reputation through the transition to private status.

However, these factors are extremely difficult to measure in financial terms. At best, they can be measured in terms of a scorecard or league table comparing one organisation with another. Comparisons such as these have their merits but they do not help us in determining the financial value of corporate reputation.

It is incredibly hard to relate a corporate branding campaign to the bottom line. However, if it is recognised that all reputation-building activities are constituents of the corporate brand, then Interbrand's concept of corporate brand value can provide some clarity. The role of the corporate brand is to provide a level of demand and security of demand that the organisation would otherwise not enjoy. For example, Coca-Cola would still be the same fizzy soda if it weren't called Coca-Cola, but would the company sell as much and could it be certain of selling as much in the future?

Interbrand's methodology developed over the last ten years has been used to value over 2,000 product and corporate brands with an aggregate value of hundreds of billions of dollars. The methodology has been used for many purposes from mergers and acquisitions through to brand licensing and government submissions. It has been accepted by a variety of institutes, governing bodies and standard-setters around the world, including the Big Five audit firms, stock exchanges, the Inland Revenue, the IRS in the US and the High Courts, and most recently has been given credence by the UK Accounting Standards Board in its Financial Reporting Standard 11.

ART AND SCIENCE

Nonetheless, the valuation of brands is still a relatively new concept. There is no active market in brands as there is with stocks and shares or real estate. Brand valuation is without question partly art and partly science. Judgement is involved just as it is for the valuation of any other asset, tangible or intangible. Specialised knowledge of marketing, accounting and trademark law is required to ensure that the correct blend of professional skills is present. Any brand valuation method has to take into account a wide variety of data, both factual and qualitative.

METHODOLOGY

Most financial analysts today value businesses on the basis of the free cash flows they produce discounted back to a net present value. A similar approach can be used for brands. The cash flows produced by the brand are discounted to their present value using a discount rate that reflects the riskiness of those cash flows being realised.

A brand is valuable because of the economic benefits it generates. The task, then, is to assess what earnings will be created by the corporate brand in the future and then to identify an appropriate discount rate to apply to the brand cash flows that have been forecast. The following approach breaks down into three tiers:

■ *Financial Analysis to yield a profit and loss forecast which is adjusted to approximate to free cash flow over time; a charge to remunerate the tangible capital is made, leaving the residual earnings attributable to the intangible assets operating in the business.*

■ *Role of Branding Analysis to determine the importance and role of the brand; by applying the Role of Brand percentage to intangible earnings, the earnings attributable to the corporate brand can be identified.*

■ *Brand Strength Analysis to assess the potential strength and security of the corporate brand franchise and from which an appropriate discount rate is derived to calculate the Net Present Value of brand earnings, ie. the value of the corporate brand.*

So what are corporate brand earnings? This is the key to the whole subject of valuation of corporate brands and reputation. It is clear that business earnings are derived from three types of assets – tangible, brands (both corporate and product brands) and other intangibles. The brand valuer's task in this case is to identify what proportion of the earnings can be attributed to the corporate brand.

The first step is to determine the forecast business earnings and then allocate a charge for the tangible capital employed. This charge represents the expected return on tangible assets in the absence of any intangibles. By examining such measures as the long-term cost of debt and the company's own cost of capital, a rate can be determined for rewarding tangible capital. The precise figure depends on the profile of the brand owner and the dynamics of the market in which the brand owner is operating. After deducting this charge from the business earnings we have, by definition, the return on the intangibles. This represents the earnings from all intangibles operating in the business.

THE ROLE OF THE CORPORATE BRAND

The corporate brand is one of the intangible assets that is deployed in the business, but there may well be others such as distribution networks, customer databases, management skills, patents, supplier contracts as well as other brands.

Some businesses have a broad spectrum of intangible assets, others have comparatively few. The difference can be seen by comparing different activities. For example, an oil company selling fuel through a retail site has a great many intangible assets at play. Marketing Shell lubricants, on the other hand, involves little other than the brand. In this product category Shell relies almost exclusively on its brand at the intangible level. The brand therefore plays a strong role in the mix of intangible assets deployed, arguably an overwhelmingly important role.

Customers are less able to make a rational purchase decision in the case of lubricants compared with their choice of retail petrol, and therefore rely on the brand to communicate the values required to encourage their purchase choice. Where there are no other intangibles operating, or if those that do exist are dependent on the brand, it can be argued that brand earnings make up virtually 100 per cent of intangible earnings.

Interbrand has developed a proprietary process for assessing what proportion of the intangible earnings of a business relate to the brand as opposed to the other intangible assets of the business. This is a particularly interesting – and difficult – process when dealing with the different product segments and geographical markets in which some corporate brands operate. For example, Shell will sell not just retail petrol and lubricants but also high-grade aviation fuel and chemicals, all of which bear the corporate brand. In addition, Shell will sell these products in several markets around the world. Customer reaction to the corporate brand will not be the same across products or geographical markets. Hence, the most sensitive corporate brand valuations will segment the brand into different products and geographical markets.

THE ASSESSMENT PROCESS

There are two distinct steps in assessing the role that branding plays. The first is to identify the drivers of demand in the business and to weight them according to their relative importance.

The second is to ask: to what extent does the brand contribute towards the success of each driver? One of the best tests to apply during this analysis is to consider how effective or otherwise the driver would be were the brand to be taken away. If the driver would be just as effective without the brand then this is a fairly strong indication that the brand has no role. If, on the other hand, the finding is that the driver would be rendered ineffective, then it suggests that the brand plays a very strong role. Clearly this process is one that relies to some degree on judgement and expertise.

One way of reducing subjectivity is to ensure that the valuer refers to independent market research to assist in this task. The earnings attributable to the brand are derived by expressing the role of the brand as a percentage of intangible earnings.

STRENGTH OF THE CORPORATE BRAND

The next task is to identify what discount rate should be applied to the forecast brand cash flows. To do this the risk profile of the brand needs to be analysed in considerable detail.

Two brands that display identical future cash flows may have completely different values. If one is a powerful, well-established market leader and the other is a highly fashionable brand launched only last year, it is the well-established market leader that would have the greater value. This is because the risk profile of the new brand is much greater than that of the more established, proven market leader. The value of a brand reflects not only what earnings it is capable of generating in the future but also the likelihood of those earnings actually being realised.

The brand's strength is the primary determinant of its risk profile as a marketing asset. The stronger the brand, the less the risk that its future cash flows will not be realised. The weaker the brand, the less secure those cash flows become.

The ability of a brand to weather a crisis is testimony to its strength as an asset. This is particularly true of corporate brands as there is no great distinction between the product reputation and the corporate reputation. Take for example Source Perrier, which suffered very bad publicity in 1990 as a result of a benzene contamination in some of its bottles. The company reacted by recalling, at substantial cost, all of its outstanding stock from all over the world. Although some argued that this was an overreaction, this step was necessary to maintain the value of the product brand and the reputation of the corporate brand. Perrier's strategy was vindicated when the brand regained much of its original market share very quickly after it was reintroduced a few weeks later.

The strength of the corporate brand is assessed relative to competitors as well as to a notional "ideal" risk-free brand. The brand is scored against seven key dimensions, which are weighted for their relative contribution to the ideal with reference to clearly established guidelines. These dimensions measure the degree to which the brand operates in a buoyant market; its longevity and stability; its leadership qualities; its penetration into different geographical markets; the level of support and protection it is afforded and so on. Once again the level of judgement is mitigated by reference to market research data, consumer surveys and key statistics such as advertising expenditure, share of voice, share of mind and share of market. The scores for each dimension are aggregated to give a percentage score for brand strength.

Once the brand strength score is known, the next task is to translate it into an appropriate discount rate. The relationship between brand strength and brand value is not linear. A totally new brand is highly vulnerable, and any cash flows forecast for it must be viewed with considerable care. A very high discount rate would be applied in such instances because there can be little, if any, confidence that the brand will realise its forecast cash flows. At the other end of the scale, once the brand is a dominant player in the market, there are diminishing marginal returns. It becomes irrelevant how much more support is put behind it, because its risk profile does not improve very much. A brand like Coca-Cola is a very strong brand already and such an asset might be compared to other "risk-free" assets like index-linked government bonds.

The relationship between brand strength and brand value therefore follows a normal distribution and can be represented graphically by an S-shaped curve. The calculation of brand value is effected by applying the discount rate identified during the Brand Strength analysis to the future brand cash flows identified during the Financial and Role of Branding analyses.

CONCLUSION

Attempting to put a value on corporate reputation is not easy. But that does not mean that it should not be attempted. Ten years ago, when Interbrand pioneered the valuation of product brands, many believed that it could not be done. However, today even the hidebound accountancy standard-setters have accepted that it is possible to value brands in a reliable manner.

A few years ago the brand managers and marketing directors who were charged with managing product brands thought that they could manage the asset without measuring it. Now they accept that brand valuation, brand performance measurement and brand accountability are essential parts of their duties.

Already we are seeing the same change affecting the managers of corporate reputation. Similarly, the development and application of techniques for valuing corporate brands and corporate reputation are now being properly addressed. This will no longer be seen as an interesting academic exercise but as an essential part of the work of reputation management.

Chapter 4

The danger of going to law

Litigation is a fact of life for UK companies and their directors. But Michael Smyth, partner, Clifford Chance, warns that when defending corporate reputations, the legal process can present a threat as well as an opportunity

Going to court to restore your good name is not like collecting a debt. More often than not, therefore, the urge to sue should be resisted. This chapter explains why.

REPUTATIONS IN CRISIS

No two crises are the same. The imperatives when dealing with them will differ, depending on the context. A crisis could, for example, involve:

- Consumers
  Here the need is to restore customer confidence as soon as possible. This may not be straightforward. In 1982, Johnson & Johnson recalled the drug Tylenol after some capsules were deliberately impregnated with cyanide by an extortionist. Anyone doubting the high profile of such incidents should reflect that that story is believed (remarkably) to have generated more press coverage than the Watergate affair.

- The environment
  The primary objective here is to stop or limit the pollution, although there may also be a direct impact on the bottom line, as found by Union Carbide, the US company that lost 27 per cent of its value within 24 hours of the leak at its Bhopal plant in India in 1984.

■ Fraud
In this context the key objective is to meet the reasonable concerns of regulators and cap the financial exposure as quickly as possible.

■ Physical catastrophe
Lives were lost in the Tylenol and Bhopal cases, but the eighties witnessed other highly visible tragedies that badly tarnished a number of corporate reputations. These included the Piper Alpha fire, the Zeebrugge ferry disaster and the Challenger rocket explosion. The task in each case was to identify what went wrong and make sure that it did not happen again.

All these traumatic episodes shared one characteristic: they unfolded in the full glare of the media spotlight. Such scrutiny is inevitably more pervasive today than it was ten years ago.

As President Clinton can testify, many news stories first break on the Internet. Indeed, some journals even scoop their own weekly publications by announcing stories electronically – making copy deadlines increasingly irrelevant. A crisis plan that fails to take account of this new phenomenon is no plan at all.

THE LIBEL LOTTERY

It remains the first instinct of some businesses to litigate their way out of a crisis and blame the media for it. That response is often entirely misconceived, not least because the outcome of litigation can never be guaranteed.

The element of uncertainty that always exists is exponentially increased in libel proceedings, which are generally heard not only before a judge but also by a jury. Jonathan Aitken and Neil Hamilton are but two plaintiffs who would no doubt confirm the damaging consequences of defamation actions that go awry.

Little better than the outright defeat is the victory that transpires over time to be pyrrhic in nature. In 1997 McDonald's won its long-running libel battle against two private individuals who had defended themselves in person. The defendants were ordered to pay McDonald's damages and their costs and injunctions were granted against the repetition of certain statements judged to be defamatory of McDonald's. Those statements are, however, repeatedly aired over the Internet on a site which is believed to have received millions of hits. In that sense, the successful verdict obtained by McDonald's has done nothing to stifle strident criticism of the company. Furthermore, the case involved the very public disclosure of information that other companies might have wished to remain private.

TO SUE OR NOT TO SUE

A writ issued in haste can be the cause of leisurely repentance. Libel cases tend to come to trial more quickly than commercial claims, but the costs involved in either event can easily run into seven figures. The successful party, whether plaintiff or defendant, is likely to be awarded the bulk of its costs.

That is not to say, however, that the unsuccessful opponent will have the wherewithal to pay those costs. Even if the winning party does recover the fruits of its victory, it will still be faced with a shortfall, in that the sum recovered from its opponent can be up to 25 per cent less than the amount charged by the winner's own advisers.

This is sometimes aridly described as "the irrecoverable cost of litigation", and it is worth bearing in mind because it is now likely that the Court of Appeal will intervene to reduce an award of damages in a libel case of more than £150,000. In just such a case, therefore, the plaintiff could find that, even if it is awarded £150,000 (a top-end award in the current climate) and its costs, it is still out of pocket in circumstances where its irrecoverable costs are greater than £150,000.

What is more, while the company's reputation may have been vindicated by the jury's headline-grabbing award, the plaintiff will not have had an apology. For the present judges do not have the power to order the giving of an apology (although this is soon to change). Defendants may of course be willing to apologise as the price of settlement but, for the moment, they cannot be compelled to do so – a further disincentive to litigate. No company ensnared in a media-driven crisis should, therefore, embark upon libel or other legal proceedings lightly. That is not to say, however, that the tactic should never be used. There is no more public vindication than one obtained in the High Court, and such cases are usually reported widely by the media.

Furthermore, suing may assuage market concerns and staunch shareholder dissent and can be part of a wider public relations offensive. But it is a game played for very high stakes. It may show resolve and cause the media to fight shy of engaging in further bouts of knocking copy. On the other hand, it could achieve the opposite result.

ALTERNATIVES TO LITIGATION

For these reasons, many businesses are increasingly turning to industry regulators, such as the Broadcasting Standards Commission (BSC) or the Press Complaints Commission, in seeking adjudications without necessarily engaging in the high-wire gamble that a libel action can be.

However, the media regulators do not sit in judgement on allegations of libel. Their jurisdiction tends to be over questions of fairness and privacy. Over the past year, the BSC has upheld several complaints by corporations against the BBC's *Watchdog* programme and the screening of the BSC's findings can often constitute a very satisfactory result.

DANGERS IN OTHER QUARTERS

It is not just the stories that the media originate that may give rise to a corporate crisis. Frequently, the threat to a company's reputation may emanate not from an exclusive story by one journalist but from media reporting of the proceedings of regulators or other scrutineers of business.

Select Committees were, for example, once considered a worthy but arcane part of our Parliamentary proceedings. In recent years, however, they have assumed considerable public significance. Notable examples of this include the interrogation of the former Director General of OFLOT, Mr Peter Davis, and of board members of the Royal Opera House by the Culture, Media and Sport Select Committee under the chairmanship of the Rt Hon Gerald Kaufman MP.

UNDER THE SPOTLIGHT

Such inquisitions are, for those on the receiving end, every bit as stressful as cross-examination by a leading advocate. As a consequence, companies are increasingly bringing in not just public relations expertise in such situations, but also political consultants. Media reports of Select Committee hearings and Parliamentary debates will generally be protected by qualified privilege, provided such reports are fair and accurate. Suing a newspaper publisher who describes your baleful performance before a Parliamentary Committee will therefore rarely be a sensible option.

All this reckons without the global impact of the electronic media. A company's reputation may be the subject of attack not just in this country but across the planet. The popular claim that cyberspace is a completely unregulated and lawless environment is overstated. Companies that are smeared electronically can, in general terms, sue for libel just as they can if they are attacked on paper. In reality, however, the uniquely extraterritorial features of the Internet make it difficult to police and legal strategies being devised now need to reflect that reality.

Directors of a number of leading companies have recently been very publicly mauled at general meetings by environmental campaigners and Third World pressure groups. Media reports of such shareholder meetings are protected by privilege – another context, therefore, in which the media are able to publish what may be very damaging reports, substantially without fear of litigation.

THE CRISIS TEAM

Just as it is naïve to assume that crises can be approached and planned for in a prescriptive way, it is unrealistic in today's business climate to assume that a crisis affecting a corporate – what the Americans might describe as a bet-the-company case –

can be tackled without external support. A crisis can be the making of a manager, but he or she is unlikely to be able to emerge stronger at the end of the process without help from outside.

After all, the board of directors may themselves have given rise to the crisis. Where there is a financial scandal, the non-executive directors of a major public company will have little alternative but to look for assistance beyond the boardroom. In such circumstances, the involvement of forensic accountants and public relations advisers will be unavoidable.

In any event, it could be that the company's lawyer knows more about the business than a newly-appointed board member and this experience too may be invaluable. The presence of a lawyer as part of the crisis team may additionally help to ensure that those key discussions that take place in the first hours and days of a crisis attract legal privilege and as such are generally exempt from production in subsequent legal proceedings.

This is not a stratagem intended to assist those engaged in fraud. Rather, the privilege exists to enable the lawyer to advise and the corporate client to be advised in a secure and confidential way at a time when matters will be developing at a fast pace.

MEDIA CRISES

So-called media crises are anything but. These are crises neither affecting the media nor created by the media. They are crises caused by companies but which the media have seen fit to cover. This distinction is important, for British companies have, on occasion, been apt to react to reporters in a defensive and indeed hostile way. The media are not necessarily the enemy. They may, indeed, represent your best and only opportunity to get across the message that you want to convey about your company.

Even if you believe that the media are unremittingly hostile, do not assume that legal restraints, even if successful at the outset, will be effective in the long term. As British public life has shown all too frequently in recent years, the reality is that very few legal gags last forever. The mere act of trying to suppress a story may, indeed, serve only to aggravate the position, leaving the media with an opportunity to headline the feature that eventually appears as "the story they tried to ban".

The trick at the end of the day will often be to reconcile the need to accept complete responsibility (the preferred public relations spin) without admitting fault (the lawyer's nightmare) where such fault is not self-evident. Resolve that tension and the worst of your corporate crisis may already be over.

Chapter 5

Reputation and directors' liabilities

Richard Green, senior underwriter, financial lines, AIG Europe (UK) Limited summarises the key areas in which directors need to be properly protected

Financial analysts and academics are increasingly coming to recognise the strong correlation between good management practice, corporate reputation, image and financial performance.

How an organisation's management responds to a crisis or disaster – and how it handles the consequences – can significantly impact on the company's reputation, share value and long-term future and, in the case of a small company, its ability to survive. Because the stakes are so high, company directors and officers are now being held more personally responsible than ever before for the decisions they make.

LINKING GOVERNANCE AND REPUTATION

Companies have never been so exposed. Increasing consumer scrutiny, the rise of the information economy and a rewriting of the rules of commerce mean that businesses – and the people who run them – are more vulnerable than ever.

In such an environment, a company's viability can hinge on its capacity to plan for crises. From physical crises – such as environmental disasters – through to new but equally catastrophic threats like the Y2K problem or Web extortion, directors and managers need to plan and re-plan their company's strategies and responses.

Corporate reputation can be threatened by an event that adversely changes the way a company is perceived by its key audiences. Sound governance and proactive and strategic

Your reputation on the line?

Duck for cover.

 **The power in business insurance**

management practices are crucial if companies are to reduce their vulnerability to crises.

OBEYING RULES, COMMITTING TO PRINCIPLES

The need for good corporate governance has been highlighted in reports by Cadbury, Greenbury and Hampel, which have recommended increased standards of corporate governance in all companies.

These reports have led to greater awareness within the boardroom. But are the changes they recommend enough to protect a company from any past indiscretions? This question may only be answered when the economy weakens, share prices fall and companies go into liquidation – revealing evidence of mismanagement as a company's ills leave the confines of the boardroom and move into the public domain.

The onus is on company boards not only to ensure that the corporate governance requirements outlined in the reports are met, but also to go further. Good governance is more about companies complying with the spirit than the letter of these codes. As the Hampel report states:

> *"Good corporate governance is not just a matter of prescribing particular corporate structures and complying with a number of hard and fast rules. There is a need for broad principles. All concerned should then apply these flexibly and with common sense to the varying circumstances of individual companies.*
>
> *"This is how Cadbury and Greenbury intended their recommendations to be implemented. Companies' experience has been rather different. Too often they believe the codes have been treated as sets of prescriptive rules with share-holders and other interested parties only interested in whether the letter of the rule had been complied with."*

The Cadbury and Greenbury reports apply only to listed companies. However, a Coopers & Lybrand survey found that one-third of private companies intended to comply with relevant aspects of the Cadbury Code.

The need for improved governance was highlighted by a range of reported operational problems. These included 31 per cent of companies experiencing difficulties in maintaining adequate internal controls. Seventeen per cent suffered a breakdown in internal controls, and 55 per cent of these instances would have resulted in a major loss to the company had they not been dealt with by senior management.

THE LEGAL MINEFIELD

Litigation is a fact of life in today's business environment, and is likely to become even more popular as the "no win, no fee" environment develops. Hand-in-hand with the tough management decisions companies need to take to succeed in a competitive business environment go risks of financial liability for both the company and its directors.

Directors and officers of large companies are particularly susceptible to litigation. In the last decade, more than 30 per cent of directors and officers of large companies have faced litigation. The increase in successful litigation against directors and officers has led to greater awareness of the need for protection. As a result of this, more than 60 per cent of UK companies now have directors' and officers' liability insurance.

Companies active in mergers, acquisitions or divestments are twice as likely to face at least one directors' and officers' liability insurance claim, and are likely to face - on average - three times as many directors' and officers' liability claims as other companies. Tighter regulation across a range of areas - including health and safety, environmental, employment and corporate governance - is fuelling the growth in corporate litigation.

Expanding companies are exposed to the local jurisdiction of every country in which their products or services are sold. Many are operating in new environments and dealing with cultures that are very different from those they understand best. So protection and planning are crucial.

WHO SUES DIRECTORS, AND WHY?

Any stakeholder in a company can sue a director or officer if he or she feels the director or officer is guilty of mismanagement. Shareholders, employees, customers, suppliers, bankers, creditors, regulatory groups, environment and community groups or even fellow directors are all possible litigants.

The issues that can lead to litigation are as varied as the interests of stakeholders. In the UK, the following key issues are responsible for 75 per cent of all directors' and officers' liability insurance claims:

■ *Wrongful termination;*

■ *Domestic marketing issues;*

■ *Discrimination;*

■ *Dishonesty;*

■ *Fraud; and*

■ *Financial reporting.*

GROWTH CRUCIAL TO SURVIVAL

With few exceptions, investors and shareholders invest to make a profit. Any adverse movement in share price or reduction of shareholder wealth can potentially give rise to a claim.

Regardless of whether they are publicly quoted or privately owned, maintaining the status quo is not an option for modern businesses. They must either expand to meet the challenges of an increasingly competitive environment or face a rundown of their business and – ultimately – closure.

Recent surveys show the structure of many private companies is likely to change in the short or medium term. Around 37 per cent of middle-market private companies anticipate a change of ownership to finance expansion plans, and 60 per cent of large companies with turnover in excess of £250m are planning a merger, acquisition or takeover.

Directors have obligations to both existing and new shareholders, employees, suppliers and customers. The diverse interests of these groups are often difficult to reconcile, but directors are personally liable for statements made in prospectuses or issue documents. And the consequences are not always immediate: actions may arise in relation to warranties, indemnities, press statements or even marketing literature well after the event.

EMOTIVE CLAIMS

The growing range of social and employment-related legislation has spawned a significant rise in the number of claims against companies and their directors and officers. These claims are often emotive and – when high sums are awarded – can attract considerable media attention.

Employment-related claims have nearly doubled in the last ten years, and a recent report by the European Commission estimated that more than 30 per cent of women have suffered sexual harassment in the workplace at one time or another.

COMPLIANCE – A GROWING CONCERN

Many companies admit that the current EU and government regulations add up to a compliance headache. Not only do regulations take time to administer and satisfy, they also require specialist knowledge.

Investigations by government bodies such as the Department of Trade and Industry, the Senior Fraud Office, Customs and Excise and The Health and Safety Executive are, at the very least, distracting. At worst they can result in serious adverse publicity.

Companies cannot afford to treat these investigations lightly: the outcome can often depend on the seriousness with which management appears to view the investigation, and on the level of assistance provided to the investigators. If a company is prosecuted, it is almost certain to make news, placing the company's reputation in jeopardy.

CRISIS, CORPORATE GOVERNANCE AND INSURANCE PROTECTION

There is no doubt that directors and officers are vulnerable to corporate crises in today's marketplace. Crises that jeopardise corporate reputation and put directors in danger of litigation are often unpredictable, and can very quickly threaten a company's viability if not handled well.

Managers may suddenly find themselves in the spotlight. But two things mark the difference between companies likely to succeed and those that could fail:

■ *Fast, relevant and effective action can avert negative consequences;*

■ *Insurance protection can minimise the financial impact on the business and the individuals who run it.*

Both will help remove the potential for retrospective criticism of how a situation was handled and, for small to medium-sized companies, could determine whether they sink or swim.

If you require any further information on any of AIG Europe's insurance products, please complete the reply-card adjacent to page 48.

Chapter 6

How to manage a crisis

Andrew Jackson, managing director, Kroll Associates, explains how to manage a crisis and emerge with your reputation intact

Writing a "how to" is never a task to relish, since somewhere down the line someone will almost always say "I thought you knew how to..." The purpose of this chapter, therefore, is to lay down some of the basic guidelines in dealing with a crisis when it affects your company.

In the late seventies, it was Prime Minister Jim Callaghan who, on emerging from the gloom of the Winter of Discontent, was reported to have asked: "Crisis, what crisis?" According to US statesman Henry Kissinger: "There cannot be a crisis next week – my schedule is already full."

WHAT IS A CRISIS?

In essence a crisis is an event or series of events which could, potentially, damage a company, its product or its reputation. Crises can include natural disasters, man-made disasters, product recalls, sudden and serious financial problems, and closures and strikes.

Very often, the timing of a crisis cannot be anticipated. However, the first step in managing a crisis is realising that it might happen. Look at your product range, factory premises and bank accounts. Do you source raw materials that have been developed through animal testing? Are your premises on the same industrial site as a fireworks manufacturer? Don't be a gloom merchant, simply realise that in life's great lottery "it could be you". Once you have realised the potential for a crisis, then comes the task of managing it through preparation.

Casualty Surety Energy Media & Entertainment

Political Risk

Trade Credit Reinsurance

Accident & Health Marine Excess Casualty

Financial Lines

Risk Management

Risk Finance

Environmental

Aviation Crisis Management Property

Protection is Better than Cure

The risks to companies and the people who manage them are on the increase as business becomes more demanding and complex. Litigation, fraud, whistle-blowers, IT risk and unprecedented changes in the regulatory environment have made businesses more vulnerable than ever before. It is not a case of if, but when you and your business will encounter one or more of these risks.

AIG Europe provides comprehensive insurance protection for both small and large companies and their directors. If you would like more information on AIG Europe's range of market leading products, please indicate your areas of interest and return this reply card.

Name ....

Position ....

Company name ....

Company address ....

....

Postcode.. Telephone ....

Fax .... E-mail...

❏ Accident & Health   ❏ Media & Entertainment
❏ Aviation   ❏ Political Risk
❏ Casualty   ❏ Property
❏ Crisis Management   ❏ Reinsurance
❏ Energy   ❏ Risk Finance
❏ Environmental   ❏ Risk Management
❏ Excess Casualty   ❏ Surety
❏ Financial Lines   ❏ Trade Credit
❏ Marine

AIG
EUROPE

Marketing Department
AIG Europe (UK) Limited
AIG Building
120 Fenchurch Street
LONDON
EC3B 0ZY

Our lives are structured around the verb "to prepare". If we fail to prepare then even the simplest of procedures can go wrong.

If my wife and I are invited out for dinner then we engage a babysitter and book a taxi. If we fail to engage a babysitter then one of us cannot go out and lack of preparation itself may have caused a crisis. If we both go out anyway and think "it'll be alright", the risk factor is enormous and we would not be ready to deal with the possible consequences. No sane person would take risks like that in normal day-to-day life, so why take risks at work, particularly bearing in mind that you might be risking the livelihoods, and even the lives, of many people?

THE CRISIS MANAGEMENT PLAN

What most enlightened companies now have in place is what has come to be known as the "crisis management plan". While glib phrases of this kind have become the newspeak of the age, the simple language really does mean something, and that is that the company concerned has evaluated its risk exposure and is prepared for the day when potential crises become reality.

So what is a crisis management plan? First of all, it is not a rigid set of procedures that should be bolted on to a company. The crisis management plan should be tailored to the needs of the particular company – its staff, its premises, its product, its suppliers, and its customers.

It needs to be flexible enough to deal with any changes to the company, but it should be fully understood so that it can be properly applied when needed. It is not a gimmick, an insurance policy or the written equivalent of having a lucky charm in one's pocket. It is there for a purpose.

A crisis management plan has a number of parts but, as with the formulation of any company policy, in the first instance it is vital to establish your goals. These may include being able to:

■ *Demonstrate the company's concern for its staff, customers and the environment;*

■ *Foster a united front with community leaders;*

■ *Maintain the credibility of the company and its product;*

■ *Ensure that the company's position is presented clearly and accurately.*

Once the goals have been set, it is time to identify the personnel for the crisis management team. You may choose to have more than one team. For example there may be a core team consisting of the managing director, human resources director, finance director, in-house lawyer and security director. Often teams may be led by the head of the affected division, with key positions being assigned. You should ensure communication links between the various teams, team lists should be updated regularly and, if possible, reserve members should be appointed to take account of holiday or illness.

Each member of the team should be allocated specific responsibilities, and clearly defined reporting lines should be established. Particular members of the team should be nominated to deal, for example, with media liaison, police, regulators, politicians/ political bodies, pressure groups and trade unions. You should ensure that these appointed individuals have adequate experience and training to perform these duties. In addition, procedures should be written down which would allow the various potential crises to be dealt with efficiently.

HANDLING THE MEDIA

All procedures should be tailored to the specific characteristics of the potential crisis; those for an internal fraud investigation will not be the same as those required for a product recall.

There are a few points worth noting about the person appointed to act as media spokesperson, and about media handling generally. A serious crisis will inevitably attract press interest, and interviews by the media can be intimidating. Any statements made should be simple and factual.

There should be no real or perceived evasiveness. This would only add fuel to the fire and send the media into an even greater frenzy. So experience, training and the garnering of good press and community relations are absolutely crucial. Remember, you will need their help.

As well as the media there are other groups who should be, or may need to be, kept informed. At the top of the list are the shareholders, banks, investors and staff. Subject to the nature of the crisis, the list may extend to customers, suppliers, pressure groups, politicians and local residents.

One matter frequently overlooked is equipment. In the midst of a crisis people need to be in touch with each other. A reserve stock of simple things such as cellular phones, pagers, laptop computers and televisions may well prove essential.

BE PREPARED

These guidelines can never be exhaustive. The secret of good planning is to prepare thoroughly for all eventualities. Some may feel that they needn't bother, and that talk of crisis management plans is scaremongering. Think again, and think of those to whom you as a director owe a duty – the shareholders, in particular, but also the employees, customers and many others.

If a company is ill-prepared to deal with a crisis, then the simple fact is that when a crisis happens, the reputation of the company will suffer. Suppliers, consumers and investors may become distrustful and start looking elsewhere to do business. Skilled employees may become disenchanted and leave. The value of the company will drop. What may have begun as a crisis which, given good planning, could have been effectively dealt with, could end up as a crisis impossible to overcome.

In the marketplace, if cash is king, then reputation is queen. Proper and well thought-out preparation should ensure that a company's reputation remains intact whatever crisis is waiting around the corner.

Reputation.

Protection
is better
than cure.

AIG EUROPE **The power in business insurance**

Chapter 7

The role of reputation in crisis management

Communicating with customers, shareholders, employees and the media in a crisis is critical to successfully weathering the storm with your reputation intact – or even enhanced – according to David Brotzen, director of issues and crisis management, Hill & Knowlton

Every company needs to take a long hard look at the factors that could endanger its reputation and – ultimately – its ability to do business.

Sadly, too many take the view that their company is immune to crisis, and think crises are things that happen to others. But the evidence is all around us: every day newspapers carry articles describing crises that threaten to damage a company's reputation irretrievably and jeopardise its ability to operate.

WHAT IS REPUTATION?

When people say "reputation", what exactly do they mean? Reputation comprises three elements:

■ *Personality – what your company is, or the character and ethos of your company;*

■ *Identity – what your company says it is, or how you want it to be perceived, and the corporate communication activity undertaken to support its reputation;*

■ *Image – how stakeholders view your company; or the perception that key stakeholders, or audiences, have of your company.*

A company's reputation is important because it affects the way its various stakeholders behave towards it. This applies in equal measure to employees, investors, customers and the general public, and influences such key issues as employee retention, customer satisfaction, customer loyalty and investor relations.

VALUES CRUCIAL TO REPUTATION

There are two important points about reputation. First, it is a state of mind. It is a set of memories, perceptions and opinions that sits in your stakeholders' consciousness. And second, communicating with your stakeholders should lie at the heart of all your reputation-building activity. Various studies have shown that different stakeholders prioritise corporate reputation characteristics in a different order. For example – not surprisingly – investors believe financial performance is by far the most important characteristic, followed by quality of management. For customers, however, the quality of services and products, together with customer service, are the highest priorities.

CALCULATING YOUR REPUTATION'S VALUE

A cynic might ask: Why invest time in managing something which does not directly add to the company's bottom line?

But a company's reputation is its most valuable asset and is becoming more important with time. To back this up, one need look no further than how the value of goodwill in corporate takeovers has increased – from 18 per cent to 82 per cent of corporate worth during the past 15 years.

Current accountancy practices do not allow companies to put a financial value on their own corporate reputation in the balance sheet (although they are allowed to do so under FRS-10 if they are acquiring another company). However, the following models can help estimate its worth:

■ *Taking trademark licences as a starting point, analysis shows they are valued at a 66 to 75 per cent multiple of annual revenue;*

■ *Net book value to market value is valued at a 10 to 500 per cent multiple of revenue dependent on industry sector, which means an average of 100 per cent.*

However, it is important to note that these rule-of-thumb valuation techniques do not factor in individual product brand values, nor do they take account of the value that might lie in brand extension or diversification. As a result, when calculating your reputation's value, it is reasonable to conclude that a company's reputation is conservatively worth between 66 and 100 per cent of its annual revenues.

WHAT PUTS A COMPANY'S REPUTATION AT RISK?

A single event or occurrence – on its own – will rarely threaten a business's reputation. More often than not it is an event followed by poor management of the consequences that jeopardises corporate reputation.

There are, however, particular events which immediately sound reputational alarm bells. These include:

■ *Publicly aired squabbles such as high-profile boardroom "bust-ups" or libel court cases;*

■ *A public accusation of "dual standards" – increasingly as a result of the combination of global business and global media. This might result from issues which move consumers to action – such as human rights, corporate ethics, environmental matters or the perception of inequitable practices;*

■ *Loss of regulatory approval, which automatically pitches the company's reputation against that of the regulator. Examples of companies coming out on top in this type of situation are extremely rare.*

Now, more than ever before, companies are giving their people the tools to hold them accountable – vision, goals and guiding principles – and going to great lengths to publicise them.

HOW CAN YOUR COMPANY PROTECT ITS REPUTATION?

The latter-day definition of a crisis is any situation that can:

- *Interfere with normal operations;*

- *Attract close external scrutiny;*

- *Damage the bottom line;*

- *Escalate in intensity; and*

- *Jeopardise the positive public image of a company or its leaders.*

The final point is possibly the most important. So what can you do to avoid jeopardising your company's image?

The three guiding principles in managing reputation risk are PLAN-AVOID-OFFSET.

This planning/action cycle is continuous. The bank of goodwill felt towards your company by all audiences needs careful nurturing over time. Your company's ability to respond to threats to its reputation has to be developed and rehearsed. Your ability to anticipate crises and adopt procedures that minimise their likelihood will only result from awareness and commitment at all levels of your organisation.

PLAN

Not all crises are alike, but prudent crisis planners will devise templates in advance to deal with the various risks that could occur. They should assess the nature, probability and severity of each type of risk and devise a response. Each employee's role and responsibilities – from chairman to receptionist – should be established in advance, and appropriate contact should be made with local emergency services and regulatory bodies.

Research from business analysts demonstrates that most crises occur in relatively small non-core operations located a long way from head office and then escalate into wider issues, so it is worthwhile making sure all parts of the organisation are continually monitored for risk.

AVOID

Commercial crises are usually a culmination of a number of small events which, when multiplied, create a situation that threatens the whole business.

To reduce the risk of large, business-threatening events occurring, each of the smaller events should be identified and neutralised. This process of managing risk requires the buy-in and commitment of every level of management, plus an understanding of the importance of their contribution.

OFFSET

The best way to avoid risk is to build reputation in advance. A carefully planned and well-funded campaign of reputation-building will allow your company to create a "reservoir" of goodwill that will help it in the event of a crisis. It is vital to keep the reservoir continually topped up so that it can be drawn upon in an emergency.

REPUTATION IN THE CRISIS ARENA

Against the backdrop of the PLAN-AVOID-OFFSET cycle, reputation managers should bear the following factors in mind at all times:

- The importance of communication
  Reputation is at risk when a stakeholder group begins to think differently about the company. The particular commercial crisis may occur anywhere within the company, but needs to be communicated to all. Management of this process should be at the heart of all reputation protection activity.

- Viewing reputation risk "in the round"
  Because threats to your company's reputation can potentially come from any number of areas, you need to view them very much in the round. This means you need to build awareness and capability across functional domains.

- Prevention, not cure
  Building awareness of the key triggers that might threaten your company's reputation – and investing time into thinking

about how to minimise the chances of them being sparked off – should be a crucial element of your planning.

■ Putting your response in place
Having mitigated some of the reputational risks that your company might face, the next step is to build a response capability.

SEVEN STEPS TO SAFETY

We believe there are seven steps necessary to protect corporate reputation in a crisis. The first and most crucial is to identify, task and train a team of people who have the experience, authority and ability to convene at short notice, evaluate the crisis and manage it.

Because a crisis can affect many aspects of your business, this crisis team should be multi-disciplinary.

Although each crisis is different, the members of the core crisis management team should remain consistent. Team members may be put on standby if their area is not directly affected. By the same token, outside experts may be called in to join or consult with the team. A crisis team usually comprises the following experts:

■ *A team leader;*

■ *A team coordinator;*

■ *An administrative representative;*

■ *A legal expert;*

■ *A communication adviser;*

■ *A finance representative;*

■ *An insurance representative;*

■ *An IT expert, especially if an intranet/Internet will be used as a crisis management tool.*

With the team in place, the next six critical steps can be followed:

- *Build awareness – ensure team members understand the importance of reputation and can spot the signals of a potential crisis. One very persuasive way of doing this is by pointing out managers' liability in the event of a crisis;*

- *Audit your own company-level vulnerabilities;*

- *Prepare mitigation strategies against the highest-priority vulnerabilities;*

- *Plan your response to each of the priority vulnerabilities. For example, know the experts who can be called upon to help you manage the crisis;*

- *Develop your crisis response plans and prepare policies, statements and procedures that may be helpful in mitigating a crisis;*

- *Simulate, rehearse and benchmark your performance against that of other organisations.*

PUTTING PLANS INTO ACTION

The best defence strategy for any company starts well before a crisis hits and involves much more than creating a crisis plan. What is essential is quick, clear, consistent, credible, efficient, and responsive communication:

- *Quick – because you will only irritate someone if you are slow to give an answer or respond to a grievance;*

- *Clear – because your message needs to be understood, and reflect exactly what you want to say;*

- *Consistent – because inconsistent communication is like a bad foundation that could collapse beneath any stance you hope to take. You need to ensure that everyone involved reinforces the same message;*

- *Credible – because you need to understand the concerns of your audiences and respond appropriately;*

- *Efficient – because the information needs of all your audiences need to be addressed by your crisis team;*

- *Responsive – because you need to respond to the concerns of external stakeholders. One way to do this is to closely monitor media, Internet and government debate on your crisis, and enlist the support of third-party experts.*

One final tip: recognise the difference between bad publicity and a crisis and calibrate your response accordingly.

"Crisis planning did not see us through nearly as much as our sound business management philosophy," said David Clare, president and chairman of Johnson & Johnson, when the Tylenol incident killed seven people in Chicago in 1982.

According to another Johnson & Johnson executive, Roy Larsen: "Reputations reflect the behaviour you exhibit day in and day out through a hundred small things. The way you manage your reputation is by always thinking and trying to do the right thing every day."

Only by investing in protecting reputation can companies establish a bank of reputation credit to help them weather a crisis storm.

This chapter is an edited extract from Hill & Knowlton's Prompt rps (reputation protection system). The system adopts a 360-degree approach to assessing vulnerability and managing crises. It draws upon advice from experts in the fields of communication, law, finance, security and risk management, insurance, and health, safety and the environment.

For more information, telephone 0171 394 5566 or visit the Prompt rps Web site at www.promptrps.com

Chapter 8

Insuring against reputation damage

Daniel Tooley, senior underwriter, crisis management, AIG Europe (UK) Limited, discusses how companies can put secondary losses first by insuring against a damaged reputation

Companies operating in today's complex and fast-changing business environment are exposed to an increasingly diverse set of risks. For many, these risks can be divided into three distinct categories – operational, financial, and business – with different individuals in the company being responsible for each one.

Protecting the company against operational risks, such as damage to physical assets and employer's liability, is usually the responsibility of the director or manager buying insurance cover. Financial risks, including exposure to interest rate or currency movements, are typically handled by the finance director. Business risks, such as developing a new product or investing in politically unstable countries, are more difficult to manage. Responsibility for protecting the company against them usually rests with the entire board.

THE DOUBLE HIT

All of these risks can have a serious impact on the company and its ongoing viability. When an event occurs – such as a fire that damages a building and halts production – there is typically an immediate financial loss. This initial impact is usually easy to assess and quantifying the financial loss relatively straightforward. However, what is not so readily apparent is the knock-on effect – the "secondary" loss.

When an event occurs, many different individuals will have an interest in the outcome. These stakeholders include employees, investors, customers and suppliers, and each will form an opinion, fairly or unfairly, about the company and its management. The event will be assessed in two ways: what financial protection was in place – such as insurance cover and loan facilities – and how effectively the management handled the event.

Stakeholders' judgements can affect the company in many ways and over a long period of time, and might result in a drop in share price, a decline in sales, and recruitment problems. The image and reputation of both the company and its management are potentially under threat.

THE IMPACT OF SECONDARY LOSSES

These observations are backed by academic research carried out at Templeton College, Oxford. This study, called *The effect of catastrophes on shareholder value*, focused on two factors:

- *The direct financial consequences of the crisis (such as loss of cash flow); and*

- *The negative impact on the company's reputation as indicated by a drop in share price.*

The research concluded that companies that have experienced catastrophes fall in to two distinct groups – "recoverers" and non-recoverers". An analysis of the differences between these two groups showed that the negative impact on share price "springs from what catastrophes reveal about management skills not hitherto reflected in value" – meaning that the crisis triggers a re-evaluation of management. Therefore, if a crisis is handled well, the reputation of management is enhanced and shareholder value rises – largely due to the increased confidence in future cash flows.

Two factors are important in protecting your company. The first is to take out an appropriate insurance policy to protect against initial losses, and the second is a crisis plan to help protect against secondary losses.

HOW INSURANCE RESPONDS

As mentioned, there are essentially three types of risk: operational, financial and business. Traditionally, insurance has concentrated on operational risks, such as property damage and employer's liability. In such cases, quantifying the immediate losses involved is relatively straightforward: for property, it is a case of establishing the value of the property, and in liability, losses are defined by the courts. Additional losses, such as the "increased cost of working" following an event, are often covered under insurance policies. What is not covered is the impact on the company's reputation.

Financial risks can be reduced by a number of mechanisms, such as forward buying of currency, setting interest rates or purchasing trade debt insurance.

Business risks are – by their nature – more difficult to quantify than operational risks. Essentially they are the risks that arise from management decisions. They involve entrepreneurial judgements such as what products are needed, when they should be launched and in which markets. Most of these risks have, in the past, been considered uninsurable.

The insurance industry has largely concentrated on areas where "loss" can be readily quantified in monetary terms. But despite the difficulties involved, major strides have been made towards addressing business risks in recent years. However, until now, these solutions have been limited to specific events, such as the following:

■ *Political Risk insurance, which covers losses resulting from political acts such as confiscation of property by an overseas government;*

■ *Key Man insurance, which will pay the company a financial sum in the event of a key member of staff suffering personal injury and being unable to work;*

■ *Patent Infringement insurance, which covers the legal cost of defending a patent.*

Of the various types of business risk, reputation risk has been perhaps the hardest for insurers to tackle. Reputation is essentially an intangible asset that accountants and specialist firms are still struggling to quantify in monetary terms. Because of this, very little cover has been available to companies that want to protect themselves against damage to their intangible assets, brand value and reputation, and the future income these will generate. Although insurance may respond to the immediate losses resulting from product failure – such as recall costs and third-party claims – it has not traditionally provided an effective method of protecting a brand.

Also, little assistance is being offered to companies to manage incidents as they happen so that they can mitigate the likelihood of secondary losses. In most cases, the form of protection offered through insurance is reimbursement of the loss after the event. Only relatively recently has the level of protection offered been increased to include advice on implementing strategies to reduce risk. Obvious examples of this include property surveys, which provide risk reduction recommendations (such as the installation of sprinklers) and offer discounts for implementation, or contingency planning prior to a loss being sustained.

Proactive and responsive insurers understand that it benefits both themselves and the company they insure not only to offer pre-loss risk reduction assistance but also to help insured companies manage incidents as they occur, to minimise potential losses.

During the eighties and nineties, malicious tampering with food, beverages and pharmaceuticals was an ever-present nightmare for companies. In 1982, Johnson & Johnson – with no insurance cover against such an eventuality – lost an estimated $400m in sales after a malicious contamination of its Tylenol Extra Strength capsules.

Within months the insurance market had produced a policy that not only covered the lost profit in the short term, but also gave the company "rehabilitation" cover – a fighting fund to combat reputation damage and re-promote the affected brand.

Insurers also added access to specialist consultants –

investigators and public relations practitioners – that could offer advice to the insured company on softening the impact of an incident. Importantly, companies could now get help from their insurers during an incident – rather than after the damage had been sustained. While such innovative types of cover certainly helped minimise crisis damage, the crisis events to which they responded were very narrowly defined.

WHAT WORRIES DIRECTORS?

The insurance industry is only just beginning to address the business need to protect intangible assets such as reputation, brand and intellectual property, and is still several years away from developing a full range of solutions.

AIG Europe commissioned market research into crisis management among European company directors in 1996. The results highlighted several key factors.

■   *When asked what the negative consequences of a crisis would be for directors and their companies, the most common response was "poor publicity". Respondents were far more concerned about this than they were about legal action, an immediate loss in sales or a fall in share price.*

■   *When asked what types of incident would cause a crisis for their organisation, directors rated the following as the top 12 potential threats:*

1 *Computer sabotage;*

2 *Man-made disasters;*

3 *Fraud;*

4 *Marketing fiasco;*

5 *Hostile takeover;*

6 *Fraud investigation;*

7 *Threat to product integrity;*

8 *Extortion threat;*

9 *Product boycott;*

10 *Strike;*

11 *Sudden death/departure of a senior executive;*

12 *Financial restatement.*

Clearly defined insurance policies exist for some of these events: for example, money lost via a fraud may be reimbursed under a crime policy. But many of these events are currently considered "uninsurable". Most insurance companies would deem a product boycott an entrepreneurial risk, and therefore difficult – if not impossible – to insure against.

Insurers realised not only that many of these crises were uninsurable events, but also that when cover was available it only responded to the immediate losses – the tip of the iceberg. Traditional insurance was offering no protection for reputation, despite the fact that our research had shown adverse publicity to be directors' greatest fear.

But times have changed. In parallel with financial markets' attempts to push back the boundaries of the protection that can be offered, insurers are beginning to realise that classifying something as "uninsurable" is not a solution. There is a growing realisation that the industry must try to help risk managers manage all risks – not just basic operational ones.

PREVENTING DAMAGE TO REVENUE AND REPUTATION

Most companies understand the need to do the following to protect their reputation:

■ *Mitigate the loss;*

■ *Continue to manage their business; and*

■ *Carefully manage media attention.*

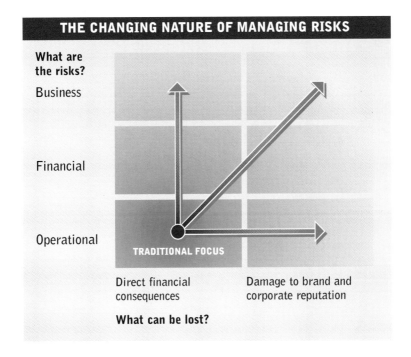

THE CHANGING NATURE OF MANAGING RISKS

What are the risks?

Business

Financial

Operational

TRADITIONAL FOCUS

Direct financial consequences

Damage to brand and corporate reputation

What can be lost?

Crucial to this is effective, comprehensive crisis planning and access to specialist resources in times of need.

AIG's Europe's research indicated that 85 per cent of directors would use external consultants to help them manage a crisis – a figure that is likely to increase if the crisis is outside the company's normal experience or threatens revenue and reputation on an international scale.

Clearly companies need to manage crises effectively – and insurance has a part to play in this. AIG Europe was the first insurer to develop Crisis Containment insurance. Drawing on our research among directors, the policy responds to a range of crisis events that can lead to reputation damage. The 16 events, or "triggers", include numerous entrepreneurial risks, such as hostile takeover, government or regulatory investigation, loss of a patent or sudden departure of a senior executive.

Because acting quickly and decisively can mean the difference between a short-term problem and a long-term disaster, the policy allows immediate access to a panel of experts who can offer advice on the best way to gain control of the crisis and mitigate reputation damage. Consultants can respond domestically and internationally, and are experts in the following fields:

- *Public relations;*
- *Accountancy;*
- *Forensic accountancy;*
- *Law;*
- *Management consultancy;*
- *Banking;*
- *Recruitment;*
- *IT;*
- *Engineering;*
- *Security;*
- *Health;*
- *Environmental issues.*

When a crisis hits, a swift public response is a company's best hope for limiting damage to its reputation and falls in its share price and consumer confidence. Crisis Containment insurance allows the insured company to call on consultants to help it control the crisis, knowing their fees and expenses will be covered by the policy. With external consultants on board, managers can keep managing the business during a crisis.

Now that companies can insure against much more than traditional risks, the likelihood of secondary losses – such as irreversible injury to reputation – is diminished. And though reputation still enjoys a high profile in the stakeholder arena but a low profile on the balance sheet, smart companies realise that it's their greatest asset – and worth protecting.

Chapter 9

Lessons from the front line

Professor Colin Coulson-Thomas, chairman of ASK Europe and author of The Future of the Organisation, explains how one major company, despite its best efforts, found its reputation under threat

Trees that have endured centuries of storms and drought can be chain-sawed in a couple of minutes. Flash floods in the night sweep away buildings and lives.

And the reputation and market value of giant corporations can be equally fragile in crisis situations. Resources of people, finance and technology as well as relationships and connections may count for nought when the unexpected happens and no-one seems to know how to respond.

Win an award and just about everyone tries to get in on the group photograph for the corporate magazine. But people are less eager to come forward in crises when the stakes are high and statements are "on the record".

TALES OF THE UNEXPECTED

Many corporations today focus almost exclusively on the normal and predictable. Processes and procedures have been developed to handle "regular" or "standard" transactions. They are examined by the auditors and periodically reviewed by process improvement and re-engineering teams simply because they cover the great majority of activities.

The exceptions are awkward and, because they are unexpected, arrangements to handle them are more limited. Many advocates of the 80:20 rule feel that unpredictable events or circumstances that may never happen are not worth spending time or money on, and the unlikely or exceptional does not merit an "agenda item". And yet unexpected events trip people up simply because no-one is prepared to deal with them. Such an imbalance of management attention needs correction. Members of the board should be forever asking "what if?" questions.

Companies with the strongest reputations and the most valuable brands run the greatest risk of loss of business and market valuation. Once word is out, for example, that Shell intends to dispose of an oil rig in the North Sea, or an allegation spreads that packages are not recyclable, even the largest of corporations can feel the effect of a consumer boycott.

Now that interest groups and lobbies are able to use the Internet to co-ordinate their plans and reach millions of individual consumers, the impact can be traumatic.

A MODEL CORPORATION

During its lifetime, whether in terms of quality awards, environmental policy or track record in the area of equal opportunities, Xerox has been a model corporation.

For example, it was one of the first major corporations to operate an environmental policy to which the board attached considerable importance:

- *Policies relating to the sourcing and recycling of paper and materials were based upon the scientific analysis of environmental impacts. In some cases, specific research was commissioned ahead of decisions being taken.*

- *Suppliers of paper were asked to provide evidence of sustainable development. The corporation was very conscious of the large volume of paper used for photocopying purposes. A centre of competence kept track of relevant research findings.*

- *Staff were made aware of their environmental responsibilities. Management teams were tasked to achieve specific improvements. There were regular reports of environmental initiatives.*

■ *New product designs made maximum economically justifiable use of recyclable technologies. Machines returned from the field were reconditioned where previously they may have been scrapped.*

■ *Considerable effort was given to alternative and socially responsible uses of surplus buildings as enterprise units. A new research centre was created on a reclaimed site. And existing structures were adapted rather than bulldozed.*

Yet, despite the care taken, unsubstantiated allegations have put Xerox's business at risk. It was subjected to hostile scrutiny, particularly in environmentally sensitive markets such as Germany. Much time was devoted to repeated and invariably successful rebuttals of various claims. But, while few people noticed small retractions at the foot of inside pages, just about every major customer seemed to spot the original headlines and stories.

FURTHER ALLEGATIONS

Another question repeatedly put at Annual General Meetings concerned trade with South Africa. As a long-standing champion of equal opportunities, and an acknowledged corporate pioneer of positive initiatives, Xerox strictly observed internationally accepted principles of corporate practice. Nonetheless, the company continued to find itself fighting off false claims that put strategically important areas of its business at risk.

The circumstances resulted from the company's sponsorship of the Commonwealth Arts Festival associated with the XIII Commonwealth Games, in Edinburgh. Xerox had been an active patron of the arts, with the paintings and sculptures at its European headquarters coming from a competition it sponsored.

In the run-up to the games, some countries decided not to participate. The view of the Commonwealth Secretariat and the Games Committee was that the planned events in Edinburgh should go ahead. Xerox, observing its obligations to various Commonwealth institutions, continued to support what eventually turned out to be an enjoyable and artistically successful event.

UNDER THE SPOTLIGHT

However, emotions in certain quarters ran high. Xerox found itself unfairly criticised in the press. Although the points raised could be countered by justification or refutation, within hours the story had been taken up by newspapers on both sides of the Atlantic. Radio and television interest soon followed. The combination of speculative newspaper reports, a major sporting event, international politics and a well-known company proved explosive.

Xerox was quickly made aware that its business with certain public bodies – local authorities in the UK and State Governments in the US – was at risk. On the strength of the initial newspaper reports, elected representatives began to raise questions in Council and Assembly chambers. Motions were drafted that all purchases of goods and services from Xerox should cease.

A crisis had arisen – virtually overnight. The stakes were high. Valued business relationships of a major corporation were being questioned. A company that had acted honourably was at risk of being economically penalised for being under the spotlight at the wrong time.

In Scotland, issues relating to the games featured regularly on the television news. Xerox found that observing codes of practice, acting within the law and doing the "right thing" did not produce headlines and soundbites that captured attention. In the interests of balance, the media tended to obtain a contrary view to whatever any corporate spokesperson might state.

However, the corporation's crisis team worked as one. Sales staff and account managers were fully briefed to communicate a consistent and convincing position to interested parties.

As a result, Xerox's business relationships held firm. The Xerox experience provides the following lessons:

- *The greater the reputation of a corporation, and the more effort it devotes to doing the right thing, the more likely it is that it will come under scrutiny and be attacked by those who set out to expose and debunk. (See chapter 3).*

■ *Events outside a company's own control can move with frightening speed. Anticipating and identifying areas of risk in advance and putting contingency arrangements in place will do much to reduce pain and anguish in the event of a crisis. Their cost may be among the best investments a corporation ever makes.*

■ *Boards must ensure that preparations are adequate. To skimp in this area is like sailing into a choppy sea without life-rafts and flares.*

■ *Secure personalities, cool heads and crisis and reputation management expertise are invaluable in crisis situations. Many spines turn to jelly and tongues dry up when the heat is turned up.*

■ *Companies that do not act with integrity run enormous risks. Never cut corners or compromise on core values. One slip among a thousand right decisions will be found out.*

■ *The truth can be communicated with conviction. Besides, after a time people get bored with distractions and speculations. Stories become stale and media attention moves on.*

The reputations of directors and boards that do not invest in risk assessment and management services are as exposed as those of corporations. Investors should endeavour to back companies whose boards and governing bodies can demonstrate a systematic and thorough approach to crisis and risk management.

Staff should be trained properly to handle exceptions and the unexpected, and relationships should be forged with appropriate advisers. External counsel should be regularly briefed. A network of colleagues and trusted advisers who understand the people, operations and issues involved and what is at stake can prevent corporate and personal catastrophe. This collective effort can ensure the company emerges with a reputation for fairness and fortitude. Finally, the areas at risk, and the people and processes for responding to threats to corporate reputation, should be regularly reassessed.

Reputation.

Make your most valuable asset crisis-resistant.

 **The power in business insurance**

Chapter 10

Reputation in the Digital Age

Business writer Nick Kochan describes how the digital media pose risks to your reputation

A Western subsidiary of a Japanese tyremaker recently turned on its Web site to find that it had been visited by so many e-mail messages that it was overloaded and no longer functioned.

The company called in investigators to make sense of this extraordinary event. It found that a trade union had used its own Web site to invite its several million members, and anybody else who was interested, to dial up the company's e-mail address and tell the management what they thought of them.

CYBER-PICKETING

The result of this "cyber-picketing" was a corporate reputation in tatters; its Web site was down, and the Web was loaded with bile directed at the company. Moreover, it was facing an expensive consultancy bill presented by the specialists who had had to unravel the mess and start up its Web site all over again.

The Japanese company had learnt the hard way what many companies learn before the hits hit the fan: the Internet is a great opportunity to communicate widely and well, with staff, customers, clients and the public. But its very openness and flexibility also pose numerous security risks which the technologists have barely conquered and most companies and employees barely understand.

Examples are legion – although many, it must be said, are apocryphal – of the abuse of the new technology. What once seemed so attractive and avant garde can now seem loaded with danger and risk.

The following instances should be enough to convince any responsible executive to build and enhance his or her company's corporate reputation:

- *The employee who gets exposed in the papers or to a competitor using the company's Internet connections to download porn;*

- *The embittered ex-employee urging insurrection in the ranks of the current staff by abusing his password access to the company's Web site;*

- *The crook who breaks into a secure area and steals privileged and valuable company information.*

Worse still, the new technology does not have to be abused to pose problems to the corporate executive seeking to protect the company reputation.

The nature of the Net is so transparent, its access so straightforward and cheap, and its range so wide that it provides legitimate and simple scope to distribute information damaging to a company's name. Answering the charges made on the Net can be costly and is frequently fruitless, but companies that fail to participate are missing a trick. While the Net is fraught with hazard and risk to a company's reputation, it is also a valuable information tool which needs managing with as much care and authority as the marketing or advertising output.

COMPANY SUFFERS WEB-STABBING

While the scare stories should not be allowed to deter the forward-looking company, the cost to a business of an unwelcome Internet intervention can be considerable.

Take the example of a US company that acquired a small business and in the process made the owner very rich. His envious employees got busy and posted on the influential Web site Yahoo Finance pejorative information about his personal life. As a result, the company's NASDAQ share price was damaged and the entrepreneur's reputation equally undermined.

Unions and embittered employees are not the only exploiters

of the wide-open Web. Pressure groups too are increasingly turning their sites to attacking corporates via the Web. This is both an easy and a cheap way of buying influence with the media and wielding power over their targets.

MCSPOTLIGHT

The most successful use of the Web in this way has been undertaken by opponents of McDonald's who won notoriety with their McLibel case some years ago. The activists set up a Web site called "McSpotlight" carrying enormous quantities of information about the company.

The site received a million hits in its first month and has continued to provide the most comprehensive database available on the Web about the company for those who dislike the business. One consultant commented: "It illustrates how a small group can reach a global audience, and say things that the company may want to contest. It also provides the pressure group with a rapid response to every company statement."

The quality and speed of comment available on the Web has resulted in its becoming a secondary news agency service for journalists and media seeking an alternative view on a story. Once regarded as "flakey", many Web sites are now regarded as authoritative sources of information and debate. Information carried on the Internet is often reflected in stories in the papers and on television. Given the sophistication and size of the Internet audience, pressure groups and companies have used the new technology to engage in debate on key controversial topics. For example:

■ *Greenpeace has set up a Web site to spearhead its campaign against exploration on the Atlantic frontier, west of the Shetlands;*

■ *Shell has used its Web sites to throw the charges back at the pressure group;*

■ *Monsanto has also set up a Web site to rebut Greenpeace's charges against genetically modified food;*

- *Project Underground is battering against what it perceives as the worst excesses of the oil, gas and mining companies via its Web site www.moles.org;*

- *A consortium of pressure groups has teamed up to create Web sites to attack whole sectors of the economy.*

The leading trade union activists using the Web are the International Trade Union Federation for chemical, energy and mineral workers. They have gained some notoriety for their ability at cyber-picketing in the US to a point where Web sites have been forced to close down.

CRIMINAL BEHAVIOUR

While such activity verges on criminal damage, other uses of the Web against companies, individuals and financial institutions are clearly criminal. Bringing the Web culprits to court, however, poses a massive problem, as the Internet has no respect for national or international borders, or jurisdictions. This was one of the reasons why raiders of the lost reputation of a large public company were never prosecuted.

The British company began to register its domain name and then aborted the process. But it left enough of its identity on the Internet that when some consultants started the registering process again some time later, they found the name had disappeared. The next day the company received an e-mail from an anonymous group of outsiders saying they had noticed the company was trying to register its domain name and had registered it on the company's behalf. The company was told that if it wanted to retrieve the name, it would cost. It later transpired that the intruders had monitored people going into this area of the Internet and seen that the registration had been started and not completed.

The intruders had, in effect, stolen the name and were now in a position to blackmail the company. It briefly considered the possibility of pursuing the thieves, until advised that they could be sitting in Venezuela, or somewhere equally remote. Finally it paid up the relatively modest sum demanded.

THE TRANSPARENCY OF E-MAIL

The Internet is full of potential potholes, which companies can fall into completely unawares. The old adage, that dangerous talk costs lives, was given validity when libellous talk about a competitor on a company e-mail was disclosed. The libelled party challenged the company and it was forced to make a financial settlement. The classic problem is that participants in Web site discussions think they are having a private two-way conversation. In fact, material posted on a company Web site is as transparent and visible as a memo circulated round the entire company.

According to one consultant: "People assume e-mail is like a conversation. In fact it is like a memo which can be forwarded to someone else with their name attached. I acquire their reputation when I forward their e-mail. But I could completely forge their identity and, saying I got this from X, forward it to Y. You would have no way of discovering if this were true, except by going back to X."

The tracking of messages and Internet access is another area for abuse, and one that lays the company's reputation open to potential damage. For those who want unauthorised opportunities to monitor internal events at a company, the Internet's "cookies" system is ready-made. This piece of software was originally designed to help advertisers target possible purchasers, but enables snoopers, such as competitors or investigative journalists, to trace executives' Internet viewing habits. If they find damaging material such as pornography being downloaded or viewed, the consequences for a company's reputation can be serious. Indeed, one US company became so concerned about the amount of pornography being downloaded that it issued an edict saying that any executive who accessed pornographic material more than one thousand times a year would be sacked. Despite the high-ended limit, 20 executives had to leave.

Management can use the same surveillance techniques to check that staff are not being disloyal or wasting their time on computer games or other Web activities. Unsupervised intruders may not only observe and exploit valuable material on a Web site, but could also add unwelcome contributions, thereby turning it into a noticeboard for every disgruntled employee or troublemaker. This can mean that the well-designed promotional and advertising opportunity presented by the Internet is turned into a forum for abusive or defamatory mail. Password systems, in theory, are outlawing much of this tampering, but companies that fail to change a password when an employee leaves run the risk of exposing themselves to so-called Web site "graffiti".

The US Justice Department's Web site was recently attacked by a hacker who replaced the logo with a swastika and the figure of Janet Reno, the Justice Secretary, with the face of a famous TV star superimposed onto a topless woman.

Mocking corporate reputation in this way is unthinkable in the non-virtual world, but in the half-real world of the Net, it puts egg on the face of the establishment and provides light relief for the hacker.

TAKING PRECAUTIONS

To guard against Web site or Internet abuse, companies should use security techniques applied in the tangible world. The requirement to carry a pass to enter a company's building is mirrored in the virtual world by the need for passwords. When data enters a computer, it should be watched as it flows through. As data leaves the company's Web site it should be checked electronically and e-mails should be examined in case an intruder has attached sensitive information like the latest sales forecasts or competitive threat data.

The basic solution most commonly recommended is the introduction of a "firewall" – a piece of computer software designed to keep out unwelcome hackers. This ensures that the holes which allow people to get in are blocked unless approached by valid, authorised users. Other software can be added to police and control Internet usage. Pieces of software will also scan every e-mail for key words like "sales". Suspicious e-mail and attachments can be "quarantined" for examination for theft, viruses or undesirable content.

Employees seeking to communicate in privacy can use a piece of freely available code called Pretty Good Privacy (PGP), which guarantees their conversation cannot be broken into.